ONE LIFE STAND

Written by Eve Nicol
Music by James Frewer and Honeyblood

Cast

Kat	**Tanya Loretta Dee**
Kit	**Edward Cole**
Momo	**Anna Mitchelson**

Production Team

Director	**Paul Smith**
Musical Director	**James Frewer**
Designer	**Natalie Young**
Lighting Designer	**Jose Tevar**
Sound Designer	**Ed Clarke**
General Manager	**Emily Anderton**

Cast

Tanya Loretta Dee Kat

Tanya trained in acting, singing and dance at the prestigious Guilford School of Acting gaining a Bachelor of Arts Degree in Acting. Tanya received the 'Highly Commended Award' for her performance as lead role Willow in *Boots* by Jessica Butcher and Sacha Voit at Vault Festival 2018. Tanya played lead role Mickey/Emma Clarke, in Futures Theatre premiere production of *Offside* by award-winning writers Sabrina Mahfouz and Hollie McNish, which toured across the UK and had a successful run at Edinburgh Fringe, Pleasance Theatre in 2017.

Other theatre credits include: *1867* (The Albany Theatre); *Marcel for Melody* (The Royal Court); *Scumbags* (Rosemary Branch) and *Long Sentences* (The Albany) directed by Ellen McDougall and Deborah Pearson.

TV credits include: playing Tanya Harvey in *Law and Order UK* (ITV), as well being seen in *The Bill* (ITV), *In the Line of Beauty* (BBC 1) and various commercials for both ITV and Channel 4. Tanya also played the lead character Olivia in the feature film, *Vehemence* by Meshack Enahoro. Tanya is also a writer and poet, and was nominated Best Debut Performance Poet at the Zoo Awards, the longest running poetry awards ceremony in London, as part of Farrago Poetry. Tanya is currently is writing her first play *Love in the time of Anxiety* – due to be in production in 2019.

Edward Cole Kit

Edward trained at Drama Centre London, The Vakhtangov Institute Moscow, Shakespeare's Globe and Hull University.

Theatre credits include: *Ten Storey Love Song, Weekend Rockstars, Mercury Fur, Apples, When You Cure Me* (Middle Child); *Kiss Me* (East Riding Theatre); *Early Doors* (Not Too Tame); *A Dashing Fellow* (Belka Productions); *A Midsummer Night's Dream, Much Ado About Nothing* (Chapterhouse Theatre) and *Sign Of The Times* (Hull Truck). Edward is a founding member of Middle Child. #hwtl

Anna Mitchelson Momo

Anna is an actor/singer currently living in Hull. She graduated from the University of Hull and was cast in her first role in Middle Child's production of *Weekend Rockstars,* which went on to a run at the Edinburgh Fringe Festival and on tour to venues including Birmingham Rep and Battersea Arts Centre.

Other credits with Middle Child include: *Modern Life is Rubbish, Jack and the Beanstalk, Aladdin* and *Ten Storey Love Song.* As well as these, she also made it to the final four in the televised national search to play Cilla Black in *Cilla the Musical.* She also performed in the Hull Truck Theatre *24 Hour Plays* and has sang at various events for them.

Production Team

Eve Nicol Writer

Eve Nicol is a playwright and director from Glasgow who has worked on new writing projects for the National Theatre of Scotland, Lyceum Theatre, Edinburgh, and Tron Theatre, Glasgow. She is the artistic director of Heroes Theatre with whom she's created theatre for fields, festivals, pools, pubs and stages across Scotland. *One Life Stand* marks her professional debut as a writer.

Paul Smith Director

Paul is a founding member and the artistic director of Middle Child. His work focuses on audiences, specifically creating an environment which attracts the working classes and those who often feel alienated by the word 'theatre'.

Credits with Middle Child include: *One Life Stand, All We Ever Wanted Was Everything, I Hate Alone, Ten Storey Love Song, Weekend Rockstars, Mercury Fur* and *Saturday Night & Sunday Morning.* He is an associate artist of Hull Truck Theatre, where he was assistant director on *The Rise and Fall of Little Voice* and *A Taste of Honey.* He graduated from the LAMDA Directing Course in 2011. He is the proud father of Ronnie, the world's greatest Shihpoo. #mufc

James Frewer Musical Director

Composition credits include: *Mixtape* (Royal Exchange); *The Hundred and One Dalmatians* (Birmingham Rep); *I Hate Alone, All We Ever Wanted Was Everything, Mercury Fur, Weekend Rockstars: An Album Play, Modern Life Is Rubbish: A Musical Manifesto, Saturday Night & Sunday Morning* (Middle Child); *Twelfth Night* (Orange Tree); *Folk* (Birmingham Rep/Watford Palace/ Hull Truck Theatre); *Get Carter* (Northern Stage/UK Tour); *Sleeping Beauty, Cinderella, A Taste of Honey* (Hull Truck Theatre) and *The Thing About Psychopaths* (Red Ladder Theatre/National Tour).

Musical director and performer credits include: *The Snow Queen* (New Vic Theatre); *Dancehall* (Cast Doncaster); *The Night Before Christmas* (Soho Theatre) and *This House* (National Theatre, dep performer).

Sound design credits include: *The Season Ticket* (Pilot Theatre/ Northern Stage); *This Land, Red Sky at Night* (Pentabus); *A Further Education, Deluge* (Hampstead Theatre); *Love Me Do* (Watford Palace Theatre) and *The Ugly Sisters* (Rash Dash/National Tour).

Honeyblood Composers

Honeyblood are Glaswegian duo Stina Tweeddale and Cat Myers, whose 2016 album, *Babes Never Die*, was described by Clash Magazine as 'one of the year's best guitar albums, a record of spite, venom, humour, and melancholy.'

Natalie Young Designer

Natalie is a set and costume designer based in Hull. She graduated from university in 2011 and has since developed her skills as a theatre designer, focusing mainly on modern and abstract design.

Design credits include: *I Hate Alone, Dick Whittington, Dancing Dead, Tomorrow Never Happens, Ten Storey Love Song, Aladdin, Till Death Do Us Part, Mercury Fur, Jack and the Beanstalk, Modern Life is Rubbish* and *Cinderella* (Middle Child); *The Tempest* (Royal Shakespeare Company/Hull Truck Theatre) and *Cosmic* (Root Theatre).

Assistant credits include: *Drip* (Root Theatre) and *All We Ever Wanted Was Everything* (Middle Child).

Costume credits include: *A Super Happy Story (About Feeling Super Sad)* (Silent Uproar).

Jose Tevar Lighting Designer

Jose is a freelance lighting designer from Hull. Jose studied MA Design for Performance (Lighting) at the Royal Welsh College of Music and Drama and has worked as a lighting technician for Hull Truck Theatre and Royal Caribbean International. Jose has recently designed for National Dance Company Wales and Middle Child.

Recent lighting design credits include: *Betty Blue Eyes* (Richard Burton Theatre, 2018); NDCW's *Alternative Routes* (Dance House, 2018); *La Cenerentola* (Dora Stoutzker Concert Hall, 2018) and Middle Child's *One Life Stand* (Tour, 2018).

Ed Clarke Sound Designer

Ed Clarke's theatre credits include: *All We Ever Wanted Was Everything* (Middle Child); *Leave Taking, The Royale, The Invisible, Perseverance Drive* and *Fear* (Bush Theatre); *A Super Happy Story (About Feeling Super Sad)* (Silent Uproar); *A Christmas Carol* and *A Short History Of Tractors In Ukrainian* (Hull Truck Theatre); *Showboat* (New London Theatre); *The Infidel* (Theatre Royal Stratford East); *Orpheus* (Little Bulb Theatre at BAC/Worldwide); *Baddies* (Unicorn Theatre); *The Realness, Politrix, Phoenix, KnifeEdge* and *Babylon* (The Big House); *Beauty and the Beast* (Young Vic/Worldwide); Danny Boyle's *Frankenstein* (Olivier, National Theatre – Olivier Award nomination 2012); *Backbeat* (Duke of York's Theatre); *The Mysteries* and *The Good Hope* (National Theatre); *The Railway Children* (Waterloo International Station/Roundhouse Theatre, Toronto); *Fatal Attraction* (Theatre Royal Haymarket); *His Teeth* (Only Connect Theatre); *Baby Doll* (Albery Theatre); *Alex* (Arts Theatre/UK and International Tour) and *Old Times* and *A Doll's House* (Donmar Warehouse).

Emily Anderton General Manager

Emily graduated from Hull College in 2012 with a BA Hons Degree in Stage Management and Technical Theatre. Whilst studying she worked freelance for various local production companies in and around Hull. In August 2012, she was appointed the role of technician at Hull Truck Theatre. Whilst in post she continued to work freelance as a production assistant and lighting designer.

Credits include: *All We Ever Wanted Was Everything*, *Ten Storey Love Song, Jack and the Beanstalk, Modern Life is Rubbish* and *Weekend Rockstars* (Middle Child).

In October 2017 Emily joined Middle Child, part time, as their General Manager. In April 2018, Middle Child became an Arts Council England national portfolio organisation and Emily now works full time as both their general manager and production manager.

THEATRE THAT MAKES A NOISE

Middle Child are a Hull-based company creating gig theatre that brings people together for a good night out with big ideas. We tell untold stories which capture the electrifying moment when the beat drops, mixing original live music with bold new writing. Our events are live and loud, making sense of the modern world.

'Middle Child claim on their website: "We will set fire to your expectations of what a night at the theatre can be." Yeah, right. But they really do.' The Telegraph

We are committed to breaking down barriers and ensuring that theatre is affordable and accessible for all. We will set fire to your expectations of what a night at the theatre can be.

We are an associate company of Paines Plough and an Arts Council England national portfolio organisation, supported by Absolutely Cultured and Hull City Council.

'Here's to FUN/LOUD theatre for ppl who don't go because the last time they went was year9 Hamlet and they didn't get it.' @Steph_Martin_ on Twitter

Middle Child are

Artistic Director	Paul Smith
Executive Director	Mungo Beaumont
General Manager	Emily Anderton
Communications Manager	Jamie Potter
Company Members	Ellen Brammar
	Emma Bright
	Sophie Clay
	Edward Cole
	Marc Graham
	Matthew May
	James Stanyer

Board of Directors
Martin Green CBE (chair), Sharon Darley, Jane Fallowfield,
Meg Miszczuk, Aysha Powell and David Watson.

Associate Artists
Luke Barnes, Alice Beaumont, Ed Clarke, James Frewer,
Maureen Lennon, Bethany Wells, Tom Wells and Natalie Young.

Middle Child is a company limited by guarantee.
Registered company number: 9921306

Middle Child
Porter Street
Hull
HU1 2JE
+44 (0) 1482 221857
office@middlechildtheatre.co.uk
middlechildtheatre.co.uk

Follow **@middlechildhull** on Twitter and Instagram.
Like Middle Child at **facebook.com/middlechildhull**

ONE LIFE STAND

Eve Nicol

ONE LIFE STAND

OBERON BOOKS
LONDON

WWW.OBERONBOOKS.COM

First published in 2018 by Oberon Books Ltd
521 Caledonian Road, London N7 9RH
Tel: +44 (0) 20 7607 3637 / Fax: +44 (0) 20 7607 3629
e-mail: info@oberonbooks.com
www.oberonbooks.com

A catalogue record for this book is available from the British
Library.

PB ISBN: 9781786825391
E ISBN: 9781786825407

Cover design: Jazz Harbord

Images p.57 and 59: *The Roses of Heliogabalus* by Lawrence Alma-
Tadema, 1888

Printed and bound by 4edge Limited, Essex, UK.
eBook conversion by Lapiz Digital Services, India.

Visit www.oberonbooks.com to read more about all our books and to buy them. You
will also find features, author interviews and news of any author events, and you can
sign up for e-newsletters so that you're always first to hear about our new releases.

Printed on FSC accredited paper

Asking for help doesn't come to me easy. That my requests for support for *One Life Stand* were met with such a generosity of time, enthusiasm, humour and whisky has made me far readier to ask for the things I need in future. Thank you to Stephen Greenhorn and the Scottish Society of Playwrights for sharing wisdom and an eye for detail; The Writing Coven, Laurie Motherwell, Conor O'Loughlin and Andy Edwards who read early treatments and scenes and whose wonderful work emboldens my own; David Greig for providing room to roam and asking the right questions at the eleventh hour; Playwrights' Studio, Scotland and Kim Allan, Hannah Jarrett-Scott, Ross Mann who lent their brains, hearts and voices to an early draft; Douglas Maxwell for lifting so many of us out of our own heads; James Frewer, Cat Myers, Stina Tweeddale for making something beautiful out of research; Georgie Mac for the gift that is Georgie Mac. But most of all to the team at Middle Child and especially Paul Smith for inviting me to join the band, widening my musical tastes and theatrical ambitions, and never being anything less than brilliant. All artists should have a company like this at their back.

Cheers, pals

x

Characters

Kat

Kit

Momo

Other humans (Silicon Wannabes, Moustache Cunt, CJ, Momma Bear, Umbros, McNugget, Street Arsehole) are shared between the company.

Tracks

The play takes place during a wet night in Hull city centre, between the hours of 8pm and 3am. Now.

Please feel free to adapt the location and references in this play to be relevant to your location and references if staging your own production.

Notes on the text

Narration is in regular type
Real time dialogue is in italicised type
DIGITAL MESSAGES ARE IN ALL CAPS
DIGITAL INTERRUPTIONS/NOTIFICATIONS ARE IN ALL CAPS
(CENTRE ALIGNED)
Song lyrics are in italic text (centre aligned)

Tonight will not educate you, answer your questions, or explain
to your parents why they shouldn't hold out for grandkids.
It can't tell you how to make your penis, breasts or bum bigger.
It can't tell you if you're straight or gay or neither or nothing or all.
It can't tell you how little or how much is normal.

A night out of the house won't solve your problems.
But it might get you off.

Kat and Kit are on a break.

[Lights down.]

---

1 //   DO EVERYTHING

*Do everything and do it well
and look hot doing it
Let me stalk myself
We've all got our little projects*

KAT	I am electric. One and a half units pitch perfect drunk. Fogging up the wet windows of the number six bus with the heat I'm giving off.
MOMO	Kat's on it tonight.
KAT	Feeling myself.
KIT	Bigger than her confines.
KAT	Potential ringing in my ears, elbow deep in a sharing bag of kettle-cooked prawn cocktail crisps. Buzzing off hangover fumes and a whiff of something more exciting on the horizon than 'send nudes' scrolling in 40-foot letters from the top of the tidal barrier.
KIT	KITTEN WITH PIZZA
KAT	DISMISS

KIT	Kit and Kat are on a break.
KAT	Kit doesn't know this yet. It'd been a properly depressing morning, throwing out an expired condom from my purse.
MOMO	Supposed to be at it all the time at this age.
KAT	Tried to make a point of it, shouting through bathroom door, a bit like this –
	Love, could you add condoms on the shopping list?
KIT	*I can't look the man in the eye when he unpacks the boxes.*
KAT	*Order it with bags then.*
KIT	*But. 'Blue Planet'.*
KAT	*Alexa, buy condoms.*

SORRY, I'M HAVING TROUBLE UNDERSTANDING
YOU RIGHT NOW. PLEASE TRY A LITTLE LATER.

KAT	*Babe, Wi-Fi's down again!* And I'm thinking, is this really it? For keeps now? Where is the promise of free love that was offered?

> *Do everything and do it well*
> *and look hot doing it*
> *Let me stalk myself*
> *We've all got our little projects*

KAT	Eight hours in wannabe Silicon Valley office but every day still starts and ends with this boneshaker of a bus juddering through city centre.
KIT	Kat works for a digital agency. Community Manager.

KAT	I hate everyone on this bus. I'd rather be in a cab. A heated seat warming my arse like a friendly cup on the bum.
KIT	*Could you transfer me a tenner to renew Netflix? There's a new season of 'House of Cards'.*
KAT	So I'm having to get the bus like a twat. For now. Something's coming.
KIT	KITTEN IN A TUB OF POPCORN
KAT	DISMISS
	Mum doesn't get what I do despite Candy Crush-ing four hours a day. Thinks a real job is stacking shelves. People can do what they love now, Mum. We've got options. You don't need to marry the first guy you kiss at the year nine disco. Drives me nuts.
MOMO	She doesn't say that.
KIT	She can subtweet it though.
KAT	YOU CAN CHOOSE YOUR ARSE, BUT YOU CAN'T CHOOSE YOUR ELBOW.
MOMO	No, that's shit.
KAT	Not my best.
MOMO	It's shit.
KAT	SAVE TO DRAFTS
	This bus has been taking me around town since I was a little girl. Escaped it. For a bit. Internship in London with an expiration date. Done everything I can to not be that little girl.

MOMO	But the worst thing a girl can do is grow up.
KAT	And I'm a bit offended, actually, that no one wants to sit next to me. Like, on this double decker filled with dicks, I'm the least desirable option. If this bus was the only surviving vehicle in a nuclear catastrophe – I'd want to fuck me first.
KIT	Feels invisible.
KAT	Worse.
MOMO	Repellent.
KAT	BUS BASTARD: IS THIS SEAT FREE? ME: NO, IT'S £1.20 FOR A SINGLE.
MOMO	Shite.
KAT	SAVE TO DRAFTS
	People will be expecting something from me though.
KIT	Juddering as bus shudders to its stop.
MOMO	Damp air hisses in, bites face, hands, anything that's exposed.
KAT	People pile on.
KIT	Swinging down the aisle is a teenage dream, dressed liked Sputnik giving her side eye with I-own-everything swagger.
	This is Momo – we'll get to her. Promise.
KAT	Try to look friendly, move my bag tighter under feet.
MOMO	Clinks like a mad alky.
KIT	Tinfoil teen swings on by.

KAT	It's only a half-empty bottle of the nice stuff from Waitrose. The kind that only comes out for senior management parties. Would've gone to waste if I hadn't lifted it. Sitting out all weekend. A small act of charity. In you pop, Sauvignon Blanc 2016, away home with me.
	I LIKE MY MEN LIKE I LIKE MY WINE. WHITE, DRY AND WITH A SCREW-OFF TOP.
	SAVE TO DRAFTS
	Can't all be winners.
	See, there's a promotion going. I'd expected an announcement from CJ over the vine leaves and chunky hummus. More responsibility, more recognition. Conferences in Brighton.
	The party had gone a bit like this:
	– and they were still logged into the brand account!
SILICON WANNABES	*Hahahahahahahaha!*
	What's the handle of the baby's Instagram, Sarah?
	You thought about names yet?
KAT	I don't have this programme installed.
SILICON WANNABES	*Going to be your turn next, Kat.*
KAT	Shut your mouth, Adil. I've been the model of a good employee. Do it all. People are waiting for me to fuck up. But I smiled and laughed at Sarah's shit speech. Put in a tenner to the collection. And one on the 'Guess the Weight' sweepstakes.
MOMO	Like a goon.

KAT	No one is more invested in this baby than me, man. No updates yet from CJ about Sarah's replacement.
KIT	KITTEN OPERATING OLD-TIMEY MOVIE CAMERA
KAT	DISMISS
MOMO	Breaks. Doors. Bundle on like a pack of wet dogs. Wifeys with wheeled shoppers like we're still in the Blitz.
KIT	School kids with Umbro bags big enough to fit a body – if it was cut into bits.
KAT	Empty seat air making me feel like an arse. Check my teeth in front camera. Clean phone light fills my face like midday.
KIT	Like a good fuck, your phone's tactile, teasing and knows exactly what you want.
MOMO	Like a good fuck, time turns into something else when you're with it.
KAT	I'd love a good fuck. GOOGLE, IS IT CHEATING TO JUST LOOK? Tinder is full of faces I do not want to sleep with. Swipe right anyway for a kick. Got it set to everyone 18-80 in a 100 mile radius. If there's a hot trawler in the North Sea, I want to know about it. Aye, aye, Captain Birdseye.
MOMO	Poor souls looking for someone to disappear into for a night.
KAT	Of course you want it you abseiling, puppy-patting, Moss Brother mountie.

Here's an idea:

10 MOUNTAINS TO CLIMB BEFORE
YOU DIE? NICHE BUT MIGHT BE
SOMETHING IN IT. PITCH TO CJ ON
MONDAY.
SEND.

KIT   Was it mentioned that Kat and Kit are on a break?

KAT   It was never ever Facebook Official, so he can't get pissy about it.

KIT   Can we get to that? Surely it's not just the out of date condom thing?

KAT   Look, I've been busy at work. Committing to something means going to parties, launches and networking lunches that you can't be arsed with and keep drinking through until it gets good.

    Do everything and do it well
      and look hot doing it
        Let me stalk myself
    We've all got our little projects

KIT   He hasn't had anything from her all day.

KAT   I've been doing a test.
Surprised to find that I don't really miss him. Uni boyfriends don't hold their own. We've got options. There's more to romance than snakebite and breakfast rolls.

KIT   He's been lobbing cute little pics her way all day.

KAT   I've been on this loop twice already. I'm staying on the six and gonna keep scrolling until something happens.

KIT	KITTEN UNDER A BLANKET KITTEN IN 3D GLASSES KITTEN WITH ITS PAW IN A BOWL OF WOTSITS
KAT	DISMISS DISMISS DISMISS
MOMO	There's got to be something bigger than cuteness.
KAT	I'm weeding past people I haven't yet muted, blocking ads for Clear Blue and bigger boobs. I FIND THIS OFFENSIVE
MOMO	Get to the good stuff.
KAT	Twenty notifications and one message. Dancer. Favourites and retweets: BOSS SENT TO SHOP FOR BOY CAKE FOR BABY SHOWER. THIS IS WHAT HE GOT. SCREAMING FACE EMOJI HASHTAGPENISCAKE
KIT	It's notifications mostly from mutuals, Mum, and there you go, there's the creep that liked the single semicolon she pocket-tweeted.
MOMO	Save the best 'til last.
KIT	Bus either speeded up or it's Kat's body that's gone into hyperdrive.
MOMO	Inbox. One.
KAT	Fuckin' yaaas.
KIT	Oh my fuckin'.
KAT	Yaaas.
MOMO	It's the one and only.

KIT	Fuckin'
MOMO	Him!
KIT	Her frenemy with benefits.
KAT	Moustache Cunt!
MOMO	Proper blushing.
KAT	Keep my screen hidden. Going to enjoy this.
MOUSTACHE CUNT	HOPE YOU DIDN'T TRY TO EAT IT IN ONE GO FULL STOP ONE SMALL X
KAT	He's such a slut. I bloody love it. Urg, but, man.
KIT	She'd done a mindfulness course and everything to stop chasing mad dreams like Moustache Cunt.
KAT	He's saved as 'Moustache Cunt Do Not Call' in my contacts for a reason.
MOMO	Have you been strong?
KAT	Mostly.
KIT	She still reads his blogs. Weekend plans with Kit? Hello?
KAT	Actual Netflix and actual chill?
KIT	Can't not have pizza and a movie on Pizza And A Movie Friday.
KAT	Fine. Leave him on read.
MOMO	Get the thrill from Moustache Cunt's pics instead.
KAT	All the usual promotional totes. Board games.
KIT	It's absolute wank.

KAT   Woah, woah, woah, hold up.
Something's missing from his pictures...
Long Blonde's gone.
Moustache Cunt's deleted her. Faded her out from his feed.
I'm going back, way back, deep into his timeline. Doing *A Beautiful Mind* to piece it together.

KIT   Where's he been. Pictures of Mediterranean squares, artisanal beers.

MOMO   Staring out across lakes. Sunglasses on.

KAT   No Long Blonde.
An opening to pick up, perhaps, where me and him left off?

KIT   KITTEN WRAPPED UP LIKE A BURRITO

KAT   Okay. That one's kind of cute. But.

DISMISS

BUZZ

KAT   CJ. Shit.

KIT   Here it comes.

CJ   GONE WITH ADIL THIS TIME. NEEDS TO SAVE UP FOR HIS HONEYMOON. SURE YOU UNDERSTAND. HAVE A GREAT WEEKEND. CJ BIG X

KAT   Bastard.
Have I even read that right? Refresh to check that I've read it right. I've poured all my time and energy into someone else's shite project. Supposed to have paid off, supposed to make sense not fobbed off with a shitting –

CJ   BIG X

KAT   Bastards.

DISMISS

KIT KITTEN WITH AN EXPECTANT FACE

KAT Oh God. Stop.
I don't need sweet nothings. I need something solid.

MOUSTACHE CUNT IN TOWN
DRINKS
GOOD PLACE NEAR MY HOTEL
SEASONAL MENU IT'S NEW YOU'LL LOVE IT
FULL STOP TWO SMALL XS

KAT Easy slut.

---

2 //   PRINKS ON NUMBER 6

MOMO CAN I COME HOME YET?

MOMMA BEAR DATE COMING AT 9.

MOMO SO, WHAT? HOME AT 11?

MOMMA BEAR MIGHT MAKE IT A SLEEPOVER DOT DOT DOT

MOMO URG

MOMMA BEAR I NEED MY SPACE MONICA

MOMO WHO IS HE? SEND PIC.

MOMMA BEAR GO HAVE FUN

MOMO DON'T GET RAPED.

MOMMA BEAR GO HAVE FUN

MOMO K

MOMMA BEAR BRING IN MILK

MOMO	Any other day, getting updates on your mum's active love life would get you right squiffy. But it's Friday. I've got the back seat of the number six to myself, feet up, brand new jacket. Could be the back of a limo being driven round town. Got a full bottle of own brand Red Bull that's half wine and a season ticket on my phone. Mobile's charging and I'm streaming Spotify.
KAT	What more could a girl want?
MOMO	COMMUNISM MEMES
KAT	You go a bit mad over your crushes.
KIT	Adopt new habits so you can go 'me too – I love that'.
MOMO	Shit my new school doesn't do Politics. Because I am properly into the socialism stuff now. Even though the Mr Grant thing is done.
KAT	Still keep them on Facebook. A catalogue of exes.
MOMO	Stag weekend.
KIT	Dressed like *The Matrix*.
MOMO	Leather look isn't hot. Nowhere near as sexy as when they're taking registration.
	SEXY STALIN SOCIALISM
	I've updated my profiles. Trying it on for size. Seeing how it feels.
	STYLE TEACUP PIGS SOCIALISM
	It's disappointing that ASOS don't sell those Che Guevara t-shirts.
KIT	Momo's headed into town.

MOMO   The big ad board in the middle of Prinny Quay is the perfect spot for selfies. It's great anyway with mirrors bouncing off the underside of the escalators, the sparkling sequined lift shaft, but when the rolling digi ad board hits something clean and medical – that's it right there. Pics come out proper boss. Neon and shadows, like something out a Ryan Gosling movie – one of the good ones.

KAT   It's a really good spot for showing off outfits.

MOMO   Then swing back home, pack it up, send it back to the depo and order something new for next day delivery. Imagine working at the ASOS depot. Be amazing. Unionise the workforce. Have them all packing parcels dolled up in sequins and glitter.

KAT   You need to keep up with new content if you don't want likes to drop off.

KIT   Her last post was pretty nice.

MOMO   Knee high socks and bunches like Britney before she was Britney Bitch.

HASHTAGGIRLSOFINSTA
HASHTAGSELFIE NATION
HASHTAGWOKEUPLIKETHIS
HASHTAGYORKSHIRELASS
HASHTAGCUTEGIRL
HASHTAGFULLYAUTOMATED
LUXURYGAYSPACECOMMUNISM

KAT   Stomach warming with winergy. Hand warming with charging phone.

KIT   Out for the night.

MOMO   Flicking between the Communist Manifesto Wiki and trying on different faces in filters.

KIT   This is Momo.

KAT   Seizing the memes of production.

KIT   In her own world.

Imagining people better than us
Expecting a world better than this
We got wardrobes full of expensive disguises
Prinks on the number 6

KAT   Settled down on corporation carpeted seats.

MOMO   Could stay here all night.

KIT   Head in her phone imagining herself being all the people on Insta where it never rains.

MOMO   SEARCH PRINKS
FILTER: FROM ANYONE
FILTER: FROM ANYWHERE

KAT   Trawling strangers' feeds in a fug of self-harm as she sits kinda lonely, kinda not.

KIT   Instagram's full of noodle limbs wrapped around each other, not in a state yet but getting there. Arched backs, peace sign and peach schnapps. Little bunny dancing girls emojis.

MOMO   When did I last get to use the little bunny dancing girls?

KAT   Bus slides into stop outside Specsavers.

MOMO   No, no, no, no, no, no.

KIT   Bubble's popped.

KAT   What's she spotted?

MOMO   Sink into my seat. But it's hard to disappear in spanking new silver foil Puffa jacket. How do you ask for help without looking a total state?

KAT   Always being told, 'Don't be a princess, princess. You're a gender traitor if you put on the damsel act'.

MOMO	But these knobs from school with their oversized bags put me into danger mode. Can I make a break for it before they clock me?
KAT	Double dicker is on the move.
MOMO	I cling to the pole, trying to slink past.
UMBROS	*Here, Mo. Going to give us a pole dance?*
	How much for a live show, Mo?
MOMO	Pushing me back with hands grass-stained and muddy, like they actually like being outside.
UMBROS	*I've got a five pound Subway voucher, Mo. Should that do it?*
	Have you seen the remix someone made of your video, Mo?
	Want to see it, Mo?
MOMO	Got their phones in my face.
KAT	Is that –
KIT	We can all recognise the sound of sex from one breath.
MOMO	Of course they have it on their camera roll.
KIT	Playing it in surround.
MOMO	Of course they do.
UMBROS	*You sound like a bag of cats, Mo.*
	A drowning bag of cats, Mo.
	Yes sir, yes sir, three bags full, sir.
	Get up on the pole then, Mo.

3 // BLUE LAGOON

ORDER #5146 ALFORNO GOURMET 173A SPRING BANK £1.00 SURGE. YOUR ACCEPTANCE RATE IS 92%. ACCEPT?

KIT   Nah.

             KITTEN LOOKING LEFT
             KITTEN LOOKING RIGHT

                ACCEPT?

KIT   Piss off.

             DISMISS

             GIF OF KITTEN LOOKING LEFT AND
             RIGHT

MOMO   Kit isn't getting through to Kat.

KAT   We'll come to that. Not much has been
             getting through to Kit lately.

MOMO   He's got problems and he wants you to know
             about them.

KIT   1) Work is knackering, properly woah-can't-
             feel-your-legs knackering. I've still got this
             arsing lump round my middle.
             2) The new booking system crashes my
             ancient phone. It's not fair that the people
             who can shell out £600 for a bit of kit can
             do more drops per shift. My service stats are
             way down.
             3) My girlfriend has been, frankly, a bit of a
             bitch lately. She's looking for a ring or a baby
             or something and I dunno which.
             I only took this job because she thought I
             could do with getting out of the house, get
             away from my own head, you know, maybe
             meet people.

KAT	All the other riders who camp out in McDonald's have a group chat without him.
KIT	Sheltering from the rain in a pack, backs to me. We're all drawn out into a crappy night by the promise of an extra quid.
MOMO	Kit licks his second eighty-nine pence ice cream cone of the night.

ORDER #5170 PREZZO 41 ST STEPHEN'S SHOPPING CENTRE £1.00 SURGE. YOUR ACCEPTANCE RATE IS 90%. ACCEPT?

KIT	*Nah.* Thank you.
KAT	Huddled by front door of the – can you even call it a restaurant? – Kit Googles for cats.
KIT	Needs it today, I reckon. She's been putting in the hours at work. Kinda inspiring. That kind of dedication. And I read a thing that looking at pictures of cute animals boosts productivity. It's our thing.
KAT	Some couples have Rome. Some have Paris.
KIT	We have Cats. Not just any cat though. Black cats. Kat feels sorry for them because apparently, statistically, they're the most likely to get run over or have fireworks shoved up them. Get a pic of a scruffy black kitten doing the mlem face, bingo, you're in-go. Didn't get why she was so mad on it at first, but the more you see something, the more you're drawn to its charms.
KAT	Needs to up his game.
MOMO	Find something new to entertain her.
KIT	Plus, it's cute.

KITTEN BEING RESCUED BY A FIREMAN

KAT   Kit's got a thing for cute.

MOMO   He's got some problems that only his search history knows about him.

KAT   1) Not even biking eight hours a day tires him out enough to get his head to shut up.
2) His phone's weighed down with pics he's not sure are legal or not.
3) He's not been able to get hard for her for forever.

KIT   It never used to be a problem. Our relationship's solid. Four years to the day next week. Solid.

KAT   But now it is A Problem.

KIT   Yeah, of course, at the start when it's all uhh and you don't know your way around each other and you're fully expecting an American in a trucker hat to jump out and, 'You've been punk'd! What an absolute jizzbag you are for thinking a smart, attractive, funny woman would ever want to have sex with you. Jerry, get the camera over here and look at this goddamn jizzbag.'

KITTEN IN A –

KAT   Delete.

MOMO   Top tip. If someone isn't texting you back, odds are they're trying to send you a different kind of message.

KIT   Or maybe she's dead. Spontaneous combustion or a lightning strike?
Would have to buy a suit and shake hands. Hope she isn't dead.

KAT   I didn't always reply straight away when I
             was in London.

KIT   I thought it would be easier having her nearer.

MOMO   Sits squeezing fat round his tum.

KIT   No idea where it comes from. Been doing
             everything right. Checked online for a
             diagnosis.

KAT   Spent full ten minutes reading over the
             symptoms of pregnancy just in case his
             paunch was containing a special delivery.

KIT   Kat's Instagram says she's active right now.

KAT   But nothing for him.

KIT   Shit. She's Trying To Send Me A Message.
             I'm having another 99.
             I love McDonald's.
             It's actually beautiful to the atomic level of
             the little paper goblets of ketchup. Every
             notion provided for. From door to till to tray
             easier, clearer and more customisable than
             things even ought to be.
             I don't even mind getting showered as doors
             open. Skittering of girls barrel in.

KAT   When did girls stop wearing heels on a night
             out? All trainers for top speed getaways.

KIT   They're looking brill. Really cute.

MOMO   99 delivered to his table by app.

KIT   *Cheers.*
             Yum.
             Girls order their chicken sandwiches, no
             mayo.

Herbivore men and carnivorous women
The history of our species
Clumsy and anxious disease mongering creatures
Disease mongering creatures

ORDER #5182 HANDMADE BURGER CO 54 ST
STEPHEN'S SHOPPING CENTRE £1.00 SURGE. YOUR
ACCEPTANCE RATE IS 87%. ACCEPT?

KIT	Open Incognito tab.
KAT	Muscle memory in fingers can stroke in the address to PornHub faster than his email password.
MOMO	Presented with a picture menu of anything you can imagine and a lot you never could.
KAT	Easy, clear, customisable.
MOMO	Knows where he is in this space. What his job is.
KAT	He's lovin' it.
KIT	Inhale flake. Slouch to the loo.
KAT	Riders all know what he's up to.
KIT	Door. Lock. Blue light to foil the junkies gives things a soft, underwater glow. Hugh Hefner lagoon romantic. Constellations of other people's spaff speckle walls like the glow in the dark stars in my room back at Mum's. Could tell my horoscope in the remnants of other people. Position my phone against tap for a super-duper, not-a-squeak, oh-so-silent wank.

Herbivore men and carnivorous women
The history of our species
Clumsy and anxious disease mongering creatures
Disease mongering creatures
Give me the same but different
Zero commitment zero commitment

KEYWORD HAIKUS

Barely legal cute
Teen girl babysitter babe
Home alone school skirt

Age play little girl
Kitty butt plug ass to mouth
Messy slut tag team

Rough baby sister
Pink double ended dildo
Cum dumpster cutie

MOMO	Living inside a dream that someone else is weaving.
KIT	*Fuck.*
KAT	He's hatin' it.
KIT	Shitting sexual anorexic.
MCNUGGET	*You alright in there, darling?*
	ORDER #
KIT	ACCEPT
	Accept accept accept.

---

4 //   GOOD GIRLS

In a post-Miley world
Our parts exist for other people's pleasure
Objects don't object
Good little girls don't get off

KAT I've been trying to have a really nice little mind wank here.

UMBROS *Here, Mo, how much does it cost then?*

MOMO I told Mum this would happen.

KAT Perfecting detail on a repeated idea of Moustache Cunt on his knees.

UMBROS *Do you think you're Kim Kardashian, Mo?*

MOMO I've got a 240 LED 18-inch freestanding adjustable ring light on my wish list for this very reason. Would never have to leave the house again.

KAT Mentally sticking his face on a porno GIF.

MOMO Pretend not to notice them.

UMBROS *You trying to break the internet, Mo?*

KAT At least, I'm trying to have a nice little mind wank here.

MOMO Don't feed the arseholes.

KAT CHANGE.ORG PETITION TO GET UBER IN HULL

Wouldn't have to sit and listen to Umbros having a go at some poor girl done up like an oven ready chicken.
They're getting louder.

MOMO Fuckin' Bluetooth speakers.

KIT	The bus is only sex sounds now.
UMBROS	*Can I get a picture, Mo?*
MOMO	I'd fuckin' bray him in if I didn't have to escape this with tags intact.
KAT	Somebody should really do something about this.
MOMO	People are actually smiling. Taking headphones out for an earwig.
KAT	Aw shite. Is it me? Am I supposed to do something?

In a post-Miley world
Our parts exist for other people's pleasure
Objects don't object
Good little girls don't get off
Good little girls don't get off
Good little girls don't get off
Good little girls don't get off

KAT	GOING TO DO SOMETHING RECKLESS. IF I'M NOT BACK IN 10, TELL MY MUM I LOVE HER...AND NOT TO LOOK IN MY BEDSIDE DRAWER.
	Excuse me?
UMBROS	*Does old cock have a more refined taste, Mo?*
KAT	*Pardon me, you're disturbing –*
UMBROS	*Did sir teach you that, Mo?*
KAT	*Some of us have been working all day –*
UMBROS	*You should come to round to practice some time, Mo.*
MOMO	Don't fall for it.
KAT	*Excuse me!*

UMBROS	*How many have you done at once, Mo?*
	Give the whole squad a go, Mo.
MOMO	Just ride it out. I'm good at sucking things up.
KAT	*Is anybody even paying any attention to me?*
UMBROS	*I've got selected for the England team, did you know Mo?*
	Mate, come on. It's Community Under 19s.
	Mate!
MOMO	Distracted! Go. Go go go go now.
KAT	Girl can move fast! She's bombed it out the emergency exit!
MOMO	Grab the red handle I've always been told not to touch.
KIT	Is that allowed?
MOMO	I'm on the tarmac and I'm off before first drop of blood from the holes in my distressed boyfriend jeans touches the ground.
KAT	Off like a silver bullet.
KIT	Um. Sorry. But we loose Momo here for a bit.
MOMO	My phone's still plugged into the bus! So if you look at my SnapMap, I'm riding merrily around town holding a daft cartoon party hat and balloon. But right now, 3D-1080p-full-HD me is somewhere in the general vicinity of Hull city centre. I don't quite know where.
KIT	You can see her down at Beverly Gate in the back of the skaters' YouTube upload. Good picture of her in Old Town almost being flattened by a biker on their GoPro. Rolling her eyes through windows of karaoke at Telstar on Facebook Live.

Blurred out in the background of Jameson
Street in *Generation Screwed? George Lamb
Investigates*, available on iPlayer.
A small, silver sasquatch loping through
other people's shots.

MOMO My only means of connection looping away
on the number six.

KAT I did a shit job with that. But I'm still waiting
on my round of applause. Umbros just acting
like nothing happened. People turning back
to their phones. What, no approving nod or
thumbs up from anyone for intervening?

KIT Kat doesn't belong on this bus.

KAT I AM BUS VIGILANTE! STRONG ARM
EMOJI! SOMEONE BUY ME A DRINK.

A swig of bag wine makes things better.

KIT A bus full of eyebrows raised against her.

Good little girls don't get off
Good little girls don't get off
Good little girls don't get off
Good little girls don't get off

KAT Oh yeah, now you pay attention.
It's alright. It's Waitrose.

KIT Pushes the bell with more force than it needs.
Lifts Momo's abandoned rose gold iPhone
from the seat.

KAT I wouldn't trust any of these dead-eyed
fuckers here with it.
My own phone pings.

ONE NEW NOTIFICATION

MOUSTACHE CUNT	FAVE
KAT	Thank goodness for Moustache Cunt.
KIT	She's not getting off anywhere near home.
KAT	Slide into his DMs with an unequivocal eggplant. No way he can misinterpret that.

---

5 //   NEON RUSH CONNECTION

KIT	My service stats took a hit but I got something even better en route back to the zone. Just the thing to keep Kat happy. Got it nestled to my chest, surprise vibrating my heart.
KAT	No more jobs on offer.
KIT	The guys on scooters get first dibs. The whole system's rigged. Jacket stick slick to me even though downpour's over. Showerproof my arse. I'm checking for something from Kat like a nervous tick.
KAT	This won't be the first delivery window he's missed.
KIT	Slept through another a job interview today. Please don't let Kat find out.
KAT	Kit's always been a procrastinator. This is not an environment in which he thrives.
KIT	Trick is to tape your headphones into your ears with Elastoplasts. Need to optimise every moment as a potential for self-improvement. Set audiobooks to double speed.

IN THIS INFORMATIVE AND HELPFUL AUDIOBOOK
YOU WILL LEARN HOW TO OPTIMISE YOUR LIFE, LOSE
WEIGHT, I CAN MAKE YOU HAPPY, SECRETS SILICON
VALLEY DON'T WANT YOU TO KNOW, A GUIDE TO
THE GOOD LIFE, THE SUBTLE ART OF NOT GIVING
A FUCK, TWELVE RULES FOR LIFE, LIFE CHANGING
ADVICE FROM THE AUTHOR OF, THE POWER OF NOW,
THE POWER OF HABIT, THE SEVEN HABITS OF HIGHLY
EFFECTIVE PEOPLE, READ BY THE AUTHOR, READ
WITH VOCAL FRY, READ BY STEPHEN FRY.

KAT   He knows the shortcuts.

KIT   You can get anywhere in town in half the
                  time if you cut down the pedestrian bit
                  around Albion Square.

KAT   But invariably Kit always goes the long way
                  round.

IMAGINE A STILL POOL OF WATER, IMAGINE A
WILD HORSE, IMAGINE A BUSY ROAD.

KIT   Shit.
                  Almost hit.

IMAGINE A BRIGHT BLUE SKY, IMAGINE AN
OCEAN, PRESS YOUR FINGERS TO THE PLACE ON
THE SKULL WHERE THESE THOUGHTS ORIGINATE.
WHY MEDITATION IS JUST LIKE RIDING A BIKE.

KAT   He's never taken his hands off the handle bars.

KIT   I'm one cold burger away from an
                  automated email written in all caps.
                  Fuck it.

KAT   It'll never go well for Kit if he always sticks
                  to the rules.

KIT   Ball sack crack against seat as I mount the
                  pavement.
                  Oohyah.

Neon rush connection
Head feels like a nightclub
Background noise
You know you deserve this

KAT   It's pedestrianised round here. People are pedesting. Making the most of the momentary break in the clouds. Souped up cars circle the edges like sharks slowing down for lads and lasses jumping out onto the road, shaking bare arses at taxis. Giving fingers. A pub crawl done up like *Peaky Blinders* giving a chorus of the Backstreet Boys. Cycling through smoking areas. An old raver's raving away on the street corner, white gloves and all the old tat. Cheered on by teenage goths and deely bopper hens. White-bellied gulls float like lost balloons. A Disneyland built by druggies and drunks.

KIT   I don't get why anyone would choose this. I've got blankets, central heating and Netflix at home.

KAT   Lights and noise and distractions and people having a good time in every crack in the road.

KIT   Chance a glance inside my jacket. Black fur shudders and stirs.

KAT   Kit is elsewhere. Look in front of you!

KIT   Woah, shit.

KAT   Brakes hit. Headphones ripped from ears.

KIT   Buggery balls.

KAT   Knuckles on Kit's handle bars.

STREET   *I've got right of way.*
ARSEHOLE

KIT	Street Arsehole with tanked arms. Pufferfish bristles bust out of polo sleeves. Making out he's harder than the weather.
STREET ARSEHOLE	*I've got right of way.*
KIT	A six-pack of these knobs with identical heights and haircuts. Fists balled against the cold or out of pure rage for a system that can't even give them a job as shit as mine.
STREET ARSEHOLE	*I've got right of way.*
KAT	Go on say 'right of way' one more time.
STREET ARSEHOLE	*You gonna run over some lass on your pedalo.*
KIT	I'm sorry, pal, okay?
KAT	Friday night's alright for fighting. Turned into a gladiatorial pit. Tuned in to what's happening before it's even happened.
STREET ARSEHOLE	*Pal? You. Delivercunt.*
KIT	Now I know why Kat's always going on at me to wear a helmet. Concrete really hurts when you're up against it. Jean-Paul Gaultier stinking fingers push my face in the overflowing gutter. I sink into it. What hits me is not hammy fists that, yeah, okay, are hitting me, but that these are the first hands I've felt for – what – days?
KAT	Months.
KIT	Well-practiced punches welcome as a massage.

35

Neon rush connection
Head feels like a nightclub
Background noise
You know you deserve this

KIT Don't put up a fight with this guy yelling at me to be a man. Just curl up and let it happen. Trying to protect the package in my jacket.

KAT Nothing's connecting. It's a pointless show.
Two bullocks fighting without a matador.
Their audience has peeled away to look for something better.
Hits fizzle out as drizzle starts up.
Punches peter away as they clock one another.

KIT Fattish and unthreatening.

KAT Kind of guys you'd bring home to your mother.

KIT Right, see, what I can't ignore is that the punch up got me wound up in a way that wasn't entirely unsexual.

KAT Just say what you want.

KIT *Wanna get a drink?*

KAT Yeah, it does sound mental.
Street Arsehole can't even be bothered.

KIT *You're not my type anyway. You fat, ugly bastard.*

KAT Kit. Abandoned. Only half-battered.
Headphones still chittering away.

TAKE A DEEP BREATH AND A STRETCH. YOU'RE DONE!

NEW MESSAGE: WARNING OF TERMINATION

KIT Trying to check inside my jacket but public lighting's never enough to see by.

Push through familiar green doors to
McDonald's full on glare.
Unzip.
Scoops out my prize from inside.
Still breathing.

MOMO   I'm back online! Swiping through grease
           on Maccy D's instore tablets. No phone.
           No cash for chips. Mum not responding
           to Facebook messages. Already been
           threatened to be thrown out for not placing
           an order. And Maccy D's is really not the
           aesthetic I'm going for.

KAT   It doesn't feel great, but the second worst
           thing a girl can do can still be effective in a
           crisis – find a guy and allow him to have his
           white knight moment.

MOMO   Schlubby guy with bloody nose is as good
           as any. Even though he's the definition of
           sketchy. But when this drip pulls out a tiny
           black speck of fur – how can you not melt?
           I'm the only one who's clocked it – that cats
           don't come in Happy Meal boxes.

KAT   Soft and a bit pathetic.

MOMO   The cat is cute too.

KAT   If you can get anyone round your finger, its
           Kit.

MOMO   Put on my Girl Voice.
           I like your cat.

KIT   *Uhh, cheers.*

MOMO   *Has she got name?*

KIT   *Eh, no,*
           Woah there, hold up. This is – what is this?

MOMO	He's a bit of a muppet. Gawping like Fozzie Bear wanting a hand up it. *Can I borrow your phone?*
KIT	*Um, yeah.* *Wait a sec.* Close the window to my grubby soul.
MOMO	His kitten flops about like an enchanted sock. Cries. More mouse than mouser. *She looks too young to be out.*
KIT	*Eight weeks, apparently.*
MOMO	*No way is she eight weeks. Eyes haven't even opened yet. She's needing her mum.*
KIT	*Gumtree said it was ready to go.*
MOMO	*Believe everything you see online?*
KIT	Tiny furball shakes from whisker to tail. Voms on the Formica. *Should I take it back?*
MOMO	*Why you asking me? Phone.*
KIT	*What you need it for?*
MOMO	*Oh my word, ever heard of privacy?*
KIT	Do what I'm told. Stop the kitten from falling over.
MOMO	Last year's model. Check the nick of this. *Ta.*
KIT	Awkward silence.
MOMO	*This is taking ages to load.*
KIT	*Um. My speed's been throttled.*

MOMO   Oh there I am. Cartoony Bitmoji in silver Puffa gurning away like an absolute plank. Where the hell am I going?
You know where this is?

KIT   *I just follow the blue ball. That's outside the zone.*

MOMO   *Well, that's where I'm going.*

KIT   She's done up like a pop star. Would probably look proper ace on a screen. But in fast food transparency she's all stilton blue veins and peach fuzz shiver on the surface of her skin.
You out with friends?

MOMO   *Meeting them later. You got a car?*

KIT   *I got a bike.*

MOMO   Bit shite. Might be alright.
Gonna give us a lift?

KEYWORD HAIKU 2

POV young first
Verified amateur loli
SFM DP

KIT   Back in blue light realness I can breathe. Girl out of nowhere – whoosh – got me on edge. I think I follow her on Instagram. State of you, Kit. Blood wipes off easy. Looks like I never took a hit except for heaviness in my bones and shame wrapping round my ankles.
Hand through hair.
Shit, piss drips.

That's supposed to be an aphrodisiac, right?
Like a tiger pissing up against a rock. Unleash
my pheromones.
God, I'm a proper cock.
Why aren't I braver? Don't want to go back
into the dark and the damp.

ORDER #5250 BAIT FISH AND GRILL 13 PRINCES
AVENUE £1.00 SURGE. YOUR ACCEPTANCE RATE IS
80%. ACCEPT?

Neon rush connection
Head feels like a nightclub
Background noise
You know you deserve this

KIT   I can do good by this girl.
                Man up, man.
                I can take her.

                LOG OUT

MOMO   *Looks like Batman. Your kitten.*

KIT   *Right.*

MOMO   *If Batman didn't have any bones. Kitten's called*
                Batman now.

KIT   *Who's your favourite Batman? I've got this theory,*
                right –

MOMO   *What?*

KAT   Called The Batman Test. For judging how
                low you can go in a partner.

KIT   *Batman.*

KAT   Kit tries to claim it as his own.

KIT   *There's this theory.*

KAT   My theory. You're looking to hit somewhere
                in the Keaton-Bale range. West – too old.

Affleck – too young. And wrong. If they say
Clooney, run. You don't stick your dick in
Clooney.

KIT   *Who is the best?*

MOMO   *'Wonder Woman' was good.*

KIT   *Yeah. Actually. It was.*

MOMO   Right. So he's a Wonder Woman kind of guy.
           Ready to go?

---

6 // MIDNIGHT

KAT   By the time I switch out of flight mode, my
           maps history places me at 1884 Wine and
           Tapas Bar at close to midnight. See, this is
           the kind of place I belong. The kind of place
           that comes with unspoken house rules.

MOMO   The pictures on Google Images look clean
           and warm, all corridors and corners.
           Gin fizz from cocktail lists.

KAT   Say what you like about him, but Moustache
           Cunt is so well-dressed, it's painful. Barbican
           tote bag and Kooples mannequin cool
           igniting in me the wonder of sunlight
           through clouds, the Sistine Chapel or seeing
           a galaxy being born. Collar bones. Arms.
           I haven't really looked at arms in a while.
           Sinews and skin. Moving. He's a shape. I
           wanna run down him like a raindrop.

               Leg touch under table
            Chaotic chemical propositions
            Chaotic chemical propositions

MOMO	At what age did you learn The Look? The Look of when it's pinprickingly clear you just want to fuck each other.
KIT	They've been carrying out this mental mental affair for forever.
KAT	There's a closeness that comes with a mutual follow. Shared jokes, flirting in public gives things a rosy glow. It's like we've gone back to when we were still good. Before it got toxic. When we still texted during the daytime and on birthdays. Nudging each other further in fantasies. Giving kindling to dull meetings and disappointing wanks.

Leg touch under table
Chaotic chemical propositions
Chaotic chemical propositions

KAT	We're bending each other's ears with ideas that monogamy and marriage isn't all that. It's all just social bondage. We're bound in ancient constructs that don't even serve a purpose. We're letting each other know we're kinky fuckers by saying that we think all of us, under it all, are all kinky fuckers. Regurgitating pontifications pulled from podcasts like we're the only ones with an iTunes accounts. Excusing and exciting each other with studies of bonobos and god knows and he's got a theory, right, that the basest behaviour happens in the most luxurious of spaces. And this is a nice place.
MOMO	Actual leather seats. Panelled walls hugging you. Lights so low so the darkness inside melts into the damp night outside window.

KAT   See this kind of chat, man. I've been gagging
to have it. It's been stuck behind lips,
dreamed behind eye lids. I've typed out
these things a thousand times online. But,
man. Vocalising feels like flying.

MOMO   Why do guys always go for a piss just as it's
getting good?

KAT   Wave him off as he goes to give himself a
pep talk in mirrors.
I log in to check cycle.
Score.
Here's the science bit, the molecules of me
are busting with oestrogen. I'm looking as
good tonight as I'm ever going to look.
If it's going to happen then it's going to happen.

GOOGLE, IS IT CHEATING IF IT ISN'T
LOVE?

If I scroll on, I might just find the answer.

KIT   KITTEN IN A BOX
KITTEN WITH PAWS UP
KITTEN MEWING
KITTEN WITH EYES CLOSED
KITTEN DRESSED AS A FROG
KITTEN DRESSED AS PRINCESS LEIA
KITTEN RECREATING THE NIRVANA
NEVERMIND COVER ART
KITTEN IN A DOUGHNUT

KAT   My phone is going frantic, a constant tremor
that shakes it out of my hands. Spins on the
table. Notifications battle one another.
I've got no time to take anything in.

KIT   despite the message being the same

KAT   and the same and the same.

KIT   KITTEN WITH SOME KIND OF BIRTH
DEFECT
KITTEN WITH AN OWL
UNICORN KITTEN
MARSHMALLOW KITTEN
KITTEN IN A BUSINESS SUIT
KITTEN IN A FLOWER CROWN
SIX KITTENS BUNDLED UP ON TOP
OF ONE ANOTHER IN A MASS OF
FUR AND PAWS AND WHISKERS

KAT   We were never supposed to last as long as we
did. Followed me home one night and never
left. Four years in and my hunch that loving
is not enough is unchanged. Cosy, sweetness,
consideration and care are just part of the
package.
I'm fractured like a Horcrux across platforms
and devices.
I like being able to box things off, man.
Being different people for different people.
Nobody knows me as well as Kit does.
And I feel shit that someone knows every
shitty thing about me. Doesn't let me forget
the parts I'm not so keen on about myself. I
can never be anyone but myself with him.

Hide the cost, shrug it off
Tomorrow's mess is tomorrow's mess
We missed the time to call it quits
Brush me up, shut them down
I don't know what to do with you

KIT   I'm someone else tonight! Can you believe
Momo's never been on a bike before?

MOMO   Just never got round to it. Assumed it would
just be one of those inevitable things that
happen, like uni or babies or Tories.

On the back of a mountain bike that's never seen a mountain in it's life, I'm soaring. Rain doesn't feel so wet when you're speeding through it.

KIT   Croggies kick ass – have you had one since you were a kid?
Or run 'til chest bursts and you can't see straight?
Used legs and arms and lungs and the things that keep you alive?

MOMO   It's kind of magic. A body moving me faster than buses. Bombing down Jameson Street. Waltzing waters in Albion Square. It's like being inside a phone around here. Or rather like when the movies want to show the inside of your phone, lights and speed and noise.

KAT   The world inside your phone is more like Steve Jobs' polo neck: black, basic and unrevealing.

MOMO   But the city is full of it.

KIT   Got less control carrying her extra weight. Almost over my handlebars when her fingers dig into my ribs, steers me into Prinny Quay. I'm cycling through the shut-up shopping centre like I'm the kind of guy who cycles through shut-up shopping centres.

KAT   It's a temple to the task of pairing you off. Get your waxes and your hair done, engagement ring on credit from identikit jewellers, chain restaurants for anniversaries then drop the kids off in the crèche and catch a romcom, reassuring yourself exactly how great a happily ever after is. I find this offensive.

MOMO   *Stop here!*

KIT	In the heart of the concourse, empty and echoing. Ad screen hovering above us.
MOMO	Best light in town! *Phone. I want to take a picture.*
KIT	*Camera roll's full.*
MOMO	*Then delete something.*
KIT	Make sure she can't see as I scroll. Don't even need to look down. Don't like having this much light on me. I rearrange Batman. *Quick then.*
MOMO	*Not yet, got to wait for the big white one to come around again. It's the best light.*
KIT	Ads loop.

PERFECTIL, BIG MAC, VODKA, VIAGRA – NOW
AVAILABLE WITHOUT PRESCRIPTION

SNAP

MOMO	*School badge in that one. I'll do another.*

PERFECTIL, BIG MAC, VODKA, VIAGRA – NOW
AVAILABLE WITHOUT PRESCRIPTION

KIT	*Go.*
MOMO	*Resist capitalism!*

SNAP

BUZZ

MOMO	*You've got a text.*
KIT	A text! Kat? No.

WARNING: DATA LIMIT EXCEEDED

MOMO	*Give us a skeg.*
KIT	*I can do it.*
MOMO	*Take a good one then.*
KIT	*But you look cute in this one.*
MOMO	*Aww. Still. More.*
KIT	*Okay. Try doing like, a little mlem face in this one.*
MOMO	Like a lot of things, a photoshoot's more fun with two.

Hide the cost, shrug it off
Tomorrow's mess is tomorrow's mess
We missed the time to call it quits
Brush me up, shut them down
I don't know what to do with you

KAT	Here we go. Moustache Cunt's swinging back my way. Wiping damp hands on red kegs. A man I could love for a night. Maybe less. *Hi, yeah, welcome back, did you enjoy your piss?* I'm weighing up if I want to go back to his. How did I get to this?
KIT	Clueless to what we're doing even though our browser history knows it was a long time coming.
KAT	Head and heart are throbbing. Need to find Moustache Cunt's weak spot to hold on to. Hello, socks. They've got avocados on them. Focusing on that he doesn't seem so intimidating. He doesn't sit back down. Drains his glass. Pops cucumber in moustache. I think I kind of hate him.

Chaotic chemical propositions
Chaotic chemical propositions

KAT   Right then, let's get on with this.

---

7 //   SINGLE EXPOSURE

MOMO   *Don't I look properly dressed to you?*

KIT   *You look woah mm.*

MOMO   *Your jacket's proper manky.*

KIT   Can't see the difference between my reflective jacket and her get up.
That'll be it.

MOMO   I've never been KB'ed from anywhere in my life and now twice in one night.

KIT   Got chased out mid shopping centre shoot by a beer belly in a lanyard. Shouting how he'll report me to my manager if he ever sees me again.

MOMO   And now denied entry to the wankiest bar in town.

KIT   Watching Bitmoji Momo having a great time, somewhere on the other side of the chandelier.

MOMO   *Looks warm in there.*

KIT   She's shivering.

MOMO   *What now?*

KIT   She's got me drifting after her in a daze. Something's stirring. Might be concussion. Might be desire. Could be hunger.

Chips?

MOMO   *Yeah. Chips.*

What does your red-hot desire look like?
Two people together; no guidance, no terms of use
It's society, not self, that screwed it up
Catastrophe takes place when you've forgotten about it

KIT   Deep-fried potato never tastes as good as
                they do with a hot girl beside you. Three Mr
                Whippies down and there's still room for
                more.

MOMO   Guy behind the till slipped me an extra
                single fish in exchange for a smile. Batman's
                flopping between us. Batter down her chin.

KIT   Sheltered between Biffas, shoulder to
                shoulder.

MOMO   Chip steam breath clouds the air.

KIT   Who knew vinegar could smell sexy?

MOMO   I'm always being told not to play down the
                tenfoot alone.

KIT   But there we are.
                CCTV cameras watch us perch on empty
                oyster cases. Documenting something that no
                one will ever watch.

MOMO   *Lads at schools, right, are always going on about*
                who'd get it, ranking us out of ten, who would
                you rather. I went to the deputy head. I did it all
                properly. Logged every time some wee nyaff raised
                an eyebrow. Slammed down my notebook. 'Look.'
                He couldn't even. Look. Like I'm some kind of
                bomb about to go off. None of the male teachers
                want to be alone with me. He had the secretary in
                with him, 'for my own safety'. Gives me some 'boys
                will be boys' shite. The men all think I'm dangerous
                and the women want to look after me. And nothing
                happens. Nothing changes.

I wouldn't take the crap you take on your bike.
You should strike. It's shite. Otherwise people will
always find loop holes to take the piss out of you.
That kind of lack of stability, it'll be the death of you.

KIT   Never have I ever heard someone talk so much.

MOMO   Never have I ever said so much in one night.

KIT   *You're a bit intense.*

MOMO   *Yeah?*

KIT   I don't really want to know about her problems.

MOMO   I know he's not paying attention. That's fine. But he's also not running away. I don't need to know any more about him.
I picked my name 'cause when you say it, you have to make a kissy face.

KIT   *Momo. Yeah. You're right. It's cute.*

MOMO   *You've got to have a style, a marker, something that stands out. Like, do you want to follow or be followed?*

KIT   She's scrolling through my apps.

MOMO   He's watching me. Like, proper watching.
You not got Facebook?

KIT   *Eh, no.*

MOMO   *How do you know when it's your mum's birthday?*

KIT   *Brings me down, you know, woah, heavy. Besides, I don't like living in a world that's been built by a bunch of guys who can't look people in the eye.*

MOMO   *I've downloaded it for you.*

KIT   *Great. Thanks.*
             She's got herself pressed against the wall of
             the club.

MOMO   Through the brick you can feel the kind of
             bassline that lives between your legs. He's just
             fanciable enough to crush on – but unattractive
             enough I'm not worried about getting knocked
             back for the third time tonight.

KIT   I give her name and school a Google.

MOMO   The whum whum whum of the club
             vibrating inside me.
             I remember going out.

KIT   *Remember? How old are you?*

MOMO   *You're mad gagging for it for ages. Then you get
             there and it's dead expensive, music's shit and it's
             full of proper kids.*

KIT   *I met my girlfriend in Sugarmill.*

MOMO   *Old school. How old are you?*

KIT   Batman coughs up a fish bone.

MOMO   *D'you love her?*

KIT   *We've been together four years.*

MOMO   *Yeah, but. D'you love her, though?*

KIT   *Too much. Too much to touch.*
             Do you ever get how it's easier to talk when
             you don't really know someone?

MOMO   *I like your eyes.*

KIT   *Woah. Alright.*

             Momo and Kit.

MOMO   Standing on the edge of something.

51

KIT	With kid drinks and chips.
MOMO	Diet Coke.
KIT	Coke Zero. More manly.
MOMO	Trying to look through windows we're too small to see through.

What does your red-hot desire look like?
Two people together; no guidance, no terms of use
It's society, not self, that screwed it up
Catastrophe takes place when you've forgotten about it

KIT	I can feel the warmth from her body all over me, even through 1 am chill. All my arteries feel one millimetre wider. My spine straighter. Slowly, tinily –
MOMO	– really, it's very sweetly, obviously –
KIT	I nudge my arm closer. We're in the same space in the air. Atoms connected.
MOMO	I stick a hand out into damp darkness. And it's met by another.
KIT	Not quite as soft as I imagined. Turns out there are hot singles in my area looking to fuck.
MOMO	*You going to say anything nice to me?*
KIT	*Um. I Googled you.*
MOMO	*Right.*
KIT	Aw shite. Awkward again.
MOMO	*Why would you do that?*
KIT	*That's just what you do, isn't it?* Balls. She's clutching Batman to her chest.

MOMO   *I bet if I search hard enough I could find something
              awful about you too. That you're a Ross in a
              'Which Friend Are You' quiz. That you follow your
              uncle on Twitter, even though he's a fascist. That
              you shared a quote with Minions all over. That you
              watched a Woody Allen movie – and enjoyed it.
              I could find as many reasons as there are sites
              online for why I shouldn't like you. But I wouldn't
              even look I don't wanna know what you've got
              beneath the surface.*

KIT   *The video – it's a bit – out there. Have you done
              anything about it?*

MOMO   *Why?*

KIT   *Because they could get two years for spreading that
              stuff around.*

MOMO   *Who could?*

KIT   *Your man.*

MOMO   *I uploaded it.
              Wanted to see what it looked like from the outside.
              I liked him. I fucked him.
              It was interesting.
              Thought other people might be interested.
              All I get is people like you pretending you've never
              followed their fanny. Freaking out when pussy
              grabs first.
              I'm going home.*

KIT   *What about your phone?*

MOMO   *Lob it in the Humber. I don't care. Chuck it in a
              fountain and let it freeze over.*

KIT   *I liked what I saw.*

MOMO   *Shut up.*

KIT   *I did.*

MOMO	*Don't see some stupid 'damaged goods' sticker over my mug?*
KIT	*You kidding?* I've found some unicorn, a buried treasure dug up from the wreckage of my head! She's unlike anyone I've ever met.
MOMO	By the way, I'm just like everyone he's ever met.
KIT	*No. I think it's cool.*
MOMO	*Thank you. God. I think it's cool. I felt good. Everybody online was proper gorgeous about it. It's real people that are the problem. I look good.*
KIT	*It's kinda hot.*
MOMO	*I think it's kinda hot.*
KIT	I don't need to know a single thing more about her.
	The first time I saw shagging, a compilation of proper – boom – sports fucking, I suppose. It's been like a flashbulb image, single exposure tattooed on the back of my skull, projected onto everything I've seen since.

FLASHBULBS

KAT	*Joy of Sex.* Top shelf. Brown paper cover.
KIT	Winamp. Woman – girl, school outfit, legs, pink, guy's marble-hard and really rattling going for it. It was a streaming video, on a loop. Just kept coming and coming and coming.
MOMO	Four pandas gangbanging a girl in pigtails.

KIT   *I've been trying to chase it, that total whoosh of
             knowing what your body can do.*

MOMO   If he was gonna murder me, he'd have done
             it by now. I think. I hope. I can't tell the
             difference between fear and horniness.

KIT   *Would you mind if I – ?*

MOMO   *Whatever you need.*

What does your red-hot desire look like?
Two people together; no guidance, no terms of use
It's society, not self, that screwed it up
Catastrophe takes place when you've forgotten about it

---

8 //   BACCHUS

KAT   This is fine. This is fine. Durex break less
             often than promises. And you really do,
             really, really want this.

             Neurologically different
             Too drunk to feel it
             Do you even want to
                 fall in love
             Do you even want to
                 Do you even
                 Do you even

             Bristling, boldness, moving towards one
             another bra on floor pants discarded and
             who took socks off and there's a finger on
             you and a whole hand wrapped around
             you. Feeling tiny so so tiny and small and
             swarmed by something, like the wind, like
             the rain, like being buried in sand, heat on
             your mound. Weight on top of you makes
             you forget the weight on top of you.

For however long this is, this is all that matters.

Teeth clink, knocked to floor, like you're caterwauling, like you you you you you're focusing everything on this grain of a thing that needs ground into, that needs worked into, that needs focus and care like threading a needle, like threading a needle, like threading a needle. Like you're a piece of grit, a bit of dirt in the treads of shoes being ground down and down.

Like the rocking chair you rode when you were eleven which still is the best ride ever.

You're deep inside yourself, filling in the spaces you've excavated for other people. This is your time, for you and you are fucking yourself. If there was a mirror above the bed – which you shouldn't put past this place – you would only see yourself in it. Moustache Whatever vampire melted out of the image. You're yourself. Every bit of you is you. Nail beds. Yours. Space between your toes. Yours. Hair follicles. Yours and you can feel every one. Each eyelash. Skin. You are the most you.

> *Do you even want to fall in love*
> *Do you even want to fall in love*
> *Do you even*
> *Do you even*

You're everything there has ever been or could be dreamed. You're water, foam, a molecule, a fragment, you are gargantuan and swelling and you want to be rung dry and here you are being fucked by pigs at the end of *Animal Farm*, at the end of a double ended dildo like the clip from *Requiem*

for a Dream. You are a fawn in the forest
caught in a moonbeam. You're the Prime
Minister and making the cabinet screw
one another. You're in a stable fuck there's
a horse. Whispered sweet nothings by the
dad in *Paddington*. You're Niles Crane and
getting fucked by Frasier. You're a Level
50 Charizard screwing its trainer. You are
Moustache Cunt and you're fucking you and
you are yeah you are yeah you are.

THE ROSES OF HELIOGABALUS

My phone wallpaper is a post-it sized sliver from a painting,
size of a billboard, on loan from a private collection.
A Victorian fantasy of Roman excess.
Flower crowns and plaits and Glossier colour palette.
Pink. Red. White. Gold.
Paint lifts off the canvas, the brush of a stroke.
It's clean, extravagant. Freshly laundered togas of skin smooth silk.
Rose petals delicately rendered over and over again fall on
intertwining bodies in orgy.
Petals in flurries hovering in air. Caught there forever. Falling a
thousand thousand times over.
Bodies with bracelets wrapped around biceps, holding skin in.
It's a wild love across marble and blankets. Solidity and softness.
Most delicate thing in it is the lowered gaze of lady boy
emperor empress watching on from banquet table but
not eating, tinge of I-want-to-have-that jealousy of those
suffocating in each cascade of rose. Feeling something they
long for but can't have pass over their entire self.

Do you even want to fall in love

KAT   There it is. There it bloody is.
Coming together. Not one after the other.
Aw fuck it. Tears.
It's happy crying, I swear, I swear.
Oh shit. Can't uncry.
Moustache Cunt's pretending like he can't see
it. Would love to tell him that it's not because
of him, it's just his cock. Just my body's
chemistry set that I've been dicking about
with. Mixing together unstable substances.
I'm still skimming on the surface of my
orgasm when he answers his phone.

59

MOUSTACHE CUNT	*Hi, sweetheart.* *Thinking of you, yeah.* *Have you tried the other blanket?* *No, sweetheart it's late.* *No, don't, don't.* *Okay, put him on.* *Ahem.* *Hey diddle diddle the cat and the fiddle…*
KAT	And he's singing this song and I'm not crying any more, I'm laughing. Burst my seams style, can't hold it down, next door's banging on the walls to get me to shut up and he's giving it –
MOUSTACHE CUNT	*…And the dish ran away with the spoon.*
KAT	Long for my phone. To text Kit I'm coming home. Fingers arch and ache to hold something. Pull themselves into empty claws. Grasping at air. Feeling nothing.

MOMO	Got his elbow round the back of my neck. Phone level with my eyes. Watching my video. Got him nuzzled into the crook of my neck. Breathing in sweat heat. Moving lips over arteries. Pulsing. Spit mixed with rain as he pours over me. In a stare-off with the screen. He doesn't even notice my fingers in his pocket. Slip out the change home. Slip round him. Staggered and stunned. Step over cobbles on the way back to the real world.

I'm absorbed into the scattering of broken
umbrellas, hen nights and pub crawls.

A brief swish of silver distracting the driver
with the dashboard cam car crash uploaded
to Mail Online.

Briefly caught in the face filter on the
Instagram story of girls looking for lost shoes.

A tiny speck on the pavement in the drone
footage of the boys scaling St Stephen's roof
for kicks and clicks.

Keeping my distance.

---

9 //   ALONE TOGETHER

Get out the house and out your head
Bodies changing fast as cities
I need the space you crawled inside
Be together and alone
Alone all together

MOMO   Eyes hurting from the depo lights, waiting for
the last bus home.
Scoop Batman out my jacket.
She's still.
Her breathing's real slow.
Hasn't mewed in a while.
I've got no phone, no Google, no answers.
Nothing to go on but instinct.
Rub her furiously, dark fur moving over
skeleton like it's not even attached.
Trying to kick start her system. Get her lungs
moving.
Chest to ear.

Come on, come on.

And then
The tiniest of breaths.
Shudder and spits up over my jacket.
I'll be keeping this one then.
It's the smallest gasp but the shudder that
goes through her small body sucks in all the
air around me.
Hold this wiggling sack of not-yet-claws close
with her purr reverberating over my heart.

I'd love to take a selfie.
Because what I've got is better than my
options in front of me.

Get out the house and out your head
Bodies changing fast as cities
I need the space you crawled inside
Be together and alone
Alone all together

KAT   Waiting for the last bus home and I'm stretching
out across two benches, all lugubrious like. Just
fucked feeling ghosting between my legs.
How do I look now?
Checking myself out in front facing camera.
Pretty good. Pretty good.
Might as well just check that lugubrious
means what I think it means.
Exactly what I thought.
Scroll to Adil's profile. Selfie with champagne

THUMBS UP EMOJI, CONGRATS ADIL

the prick.
On to vineyard trips in France. Maybe me
and Kit could take a break there.
Or I could go alone.
Search for flights.
Too expensive.

Moustache Cunt's feed.
He's an arse, yeah, but, aw man that jawline
gets me going.
Gets me proper going.
I could run a marathon and another, pull a
wreck out the ocean, write an epic. I *want* to
do something superhuman. *Can* do something
superhuman on the fizz and sherbet in my
head, vag and heart. I can be awesome. Want
to be awesome for Kit.

Try to find crumbs in the corner of my tote
bag. Still hungry.

What's that?
Rose gold iPhone.
Not my own.
Lock screen click.
Who sets their home screen to a selfie?
Totally blanked out by the offer of visiting cock.
But it's coming together in front of me like
a Darren Brown mind fuck when I hear
Umbros again and spot blimp girl waiting on
her bus.

MOMO	Six hours in and blood replaced with VKs and Despos these guys from school have gone from tolerable pain to highest alert.
KAT	She's practically in a ball in the closed-up shop front.
MOMO	Umbro acting out a remarkably acrobatic blow job inches from my face for the entertainment of his pals.
KAT	I Gene Kelly it down the concourse. Insert myself between them. *Nice coat.*

MOMO	*Cheers.*
KAT	*New?*
MOMO	*Yeah.*
UMBROS	*Oi, Mo, is this your Buy One Get One Free?*
KAT	*This idiot belong to you?*
MOMO	*No.*
KAT	*But you know them, yeah?*
MOMO	*From school.*
KAT	*Righto, let's get on with this.* His Tesco Value life story from tinfoil chick is all I need to super-fast pull up his mum on Facebook – nice looking woman – and message her about how much of a little shit her precious boy is to young girls.
MOMO	His phone's going. Ed Sheeran marimba shite.
KAT	*You going to get that?*
MOMO	Eyes turn into little loading wheels. I can hear his mum having a go from over here.
KAT	*Look, I'm mutuals with your rugby coach too.* *I could keep going. I've got unlimited data.*
MOMO	His pals are cracking up at him getting a bollocking from his mum and he's screeching at this woman about some scholarship he's owed. Someone has actually done something for once.
KAT	*Which way are you going?*
MOMO	She chums me onto the bus. We sit together for a bit.
KAT	Girl pulls a mangled kitten out from nowhere.
MOMO	*Do you like her?*

KAT   *I'm allergic.*

MOMO   She pulls my iPhone out from nowhere.

KAT   Switches it off with a click like a coffin lid.

MOMO   The last service of the night sweeping the
             streets.

KAT   The aisles and seats are filled with the
             accumulated waste of the day.
             All the people who didn't pull tonight are
             shrinking back into themselves and their
             phones.
             Checking football scores to see their team's
             lost.
             Looking through pictures of exes and ones
             that didn't even get that far.
             Faces tripping them, melting in to screens.
             Missing their stops.

MOMO   All the people who will go home alone tonight.

KAT   All the people who feel alone at home.

             Get out the house and out your head
                Bodies changing fast as cities
             I need the space you crawled inside
                 Be together and alone
                  Alone all together

MOMO   I snuggle into Batman, shaking on the edge
             of present and invisible, drifting between
             worlds. I didn't notice her get off. It's just me
             and reflections of passengers cut into ribbons
             by the tracks of water on glass.
             Alone together. All together alone.

65

10 //   YOUR LOVE IS NOT ENOUGH

The carpet's always the same
Combustible waste
Dick drunk
Your love is not enough

KIT   I dunno who lives here. Yeah, I know, me.
And Kat. But it's full of stuff passed down
from our parents. Don't recognise it as home.
My worlds are on the other side of screens.
Pick up PlayStation controller.
Put it down.
Sounds bleed into the flat from all over.
Wander through rooms with the lights off.
Try to imagine what our place might look
like to a burglar. Imagine what kind of
people might live here.
Anything mine is rented. Like my phone
contract, my music, paying off my bike on
credit. Nothing for keeps. I'm just a lump
generating interest and data.
Sink into a patch of streetlight on the carpet
like a house cat in a sunbeam. Got my face
in fibers. Totally brought down. Boom.
Flattened. Can't shake this love that got me
all soft and domesticated.
Can't move to sofa or chair or bed. Only
carpet now.
Still got Momo's hair tie around his wrist.
Elastic twang of something.
Still logged into her SnapMap.

KAT   KITTEN FLOATING AWAY IN A
BALLOON

KIT   Alive enough for Google Images then?

How to make a lust story
Say something you can't take back
The second you get sober
Falling in love with someone other than yourself

KAT   I linger on each landing. The key in the lock
would be the thing that breaks the dream.
Email to self.

UNHAPPY PEOPLE SPEND MORE
TIME ONLINE

Or more time online leads people to be
unhappy?
Send.
New reminder in calendar.

GO AND SHOUT AT A MOUNTAIN

But I meow through the letter box.

KIT   It's kind of our thing.

KAT   The biggest step I've taken today is coming
back over my own doorway.

KAT   *How did the interview go?*

KIT   *Mm. Alright.*

KAT   *Good day?*

KIT   *Standard.*

KAT   A stand-off in the hallway.

KIT   Neither giving ground.
You're home late.

KAT   *Sarah's do. Went out with guys from work after.*

KIT   *Sarah, course. Any news?*

KAT   *Didn't get it.*

KIT	*Aw balls. Babe. That's shit.*
KAT	*Yeah.*
KIT	*I'm here for you, you know.*
KAT	*Yeah, I know.*
KIT	*Whatever you need.*
KAT	*I'm fine.* *We got any ice cream?*
KIT	Get our bowls out. His and hers.
KAT	*Funny, isn't it, how no matter how much ice cream you eat, you always have room for more.*
KIT	*Like there's a separate stomach for it.*
KAT	*Right!*
KIT	*Did I get it right?*
KAT	*This is great.*
KIT	*There's too much choice in the shops.*
KAT	*Yup.*
KIT	*It's vegan.*
KAT	*Couldn't tell it's not the real thing.*
KIT	*Just thought. You know, Blue Planet.*
KAT	*Fish don't make milk.*
KIT	*The seals do.*
KAT	*This gets my seal of approval.*
KIT	*I'd like to see the version of me that came out of the water.*
KAT	*Like in Mallorca when you couldn't get back on the boat?*

KIT	*No, I mean, proto-limbs, mud skipper, splish-splash kind of me.*
	And it was choppy that day.
KAT	*Hard to climb onto something that keeps moving. I'd like to see the me that lived in a cave. Taking down mammoths.*
KIT	*But that'd just be the same as you now.*
KAT	*Meet in the middle then?*
KIT	*When we were reptiles?*
KAT	*Later.*
KIT	*First time we stood up?*
KAT	*Earlier. Tribal hominids?*
KIT	*When was that?*
KAT	*Like when humans and chimps and apes were all the same.*
KIT	*Like in the TED Talk?*
KAT	*You were listening to that?*
KIT	*Yeah.*
KAT	*I thought you were having a lie in.*
KIT	*Yeah, in bed but not asleep. I hear the podcasts you play when you're getting ready.*
KAT	*Doesn't it disturb you?*
KIT	*I quite like it. Not stuff I would seek out myself, you know. But makes you go, hmm, I guess.*
KAT	*I could leave the bedroom door open. If you wanted to listen.*
KIT	*That'd be nice.*
	I don't like the one with the guy who hates Trump though.

KAT	*Gonna need to narrow that one down, babe.*
KIT	*You know the one. Sex advice podcast. I think he's trying to get in your pants.*
KAT	*Babe, he's a podcast.*
KIT	*Yeah, but he's doing something to your brain. I can't get there.*
KAT	*You jealous of my phone?*
KIT	*Of what it can do. Yeah, I am.*
KAT	*Babe. That's cute.*
KIT	*Hey, no, I'm trying to be honest and you laugh at me.*
KAT	*Sorry, sorry.*
KIT	*It's. You know when you're in the bathroom for about a week and a half?*
KAT	*Half an hour tops, but yeah?*
KIT	*And I don't really know where you are. Because you're kind of here and kind of elsewhere.*
KAT	*Babe, you know that's daft. It's just talk. And he's married anyway.*
KIT	*Like that'd matter.*
KAT	*As well as living on the other side of the Atlantic, being gay, unaware of my existence, never mind me having zero sexual interest in him.*
KIT	*There was a caller on it the other day who sounded like you.*
KAT	*I've never called up a podcast.*
KIT	*But it was the kind of thing that I could imagine you asking.*

KAT	*What were they calling about?*
KIT	*What are they always talking about? That it's easier to open up to a complete stranger than define the parameter of your relationship with your partner. That nothing should be assumed.*
KAT	*We've never had that conversation.*
KIT	*No.*

…

…

…

KAT	I fold into his arms. Feel my tongue loosen. Speak in the language of our tribe of two.
KIT	Purring at one another. Shared speech beyond language, accent, incomprehensible to outside ears.
KAT	Alexa chimes in with a –

I'M SORRY. I DIDN'T UNDERSTAND YOU.

KAT	This here could be the turning point in our relationship.
KIT	Where we actually talk. Actually tell each other what we need.
KAT	That we come to some kind of arrangement.
KIT	Could be now.
KAT	We could do more than meow. *You're my favourite. The one to end my night with. Tell my secrets too. Make dens with.*
KIT	*You're comparing me to a teddy bear.*

71

KAT   *Yeah, and you still cry about losing Buddy in the park when you were ten. Don't pretend teddy bears aren't important.*

KIT   *Bet you wouldn't want to fuck one though.*

KAT   I put the kettle on as he does the dishes. Rain hammering windows. Tomorrow will be just as bleak.

> *How to make a lust story*
> *Say something you can't take back*
> *The second you get sober*
> *Falling in love with someone other than yourself*
> *The carpet's always the same*
> *Combustible waste*
> *Dick drunk*
> *Your love is not enough*

Can't say it to him but I can type it out. Lay it all out in an email.

I know what terms to search for but I don't know how to say it. How to apply concepts and theory to human insecurity? But I do know I shouldn't be blamed for not keeping up with rules I didn't make, contracts I didn't agree on. But I believe I've got room for more than one person to have and to hold on to. Staying like this will kill us quick or kill us slow. If I say what I want at least, I guess, I'd know. We could figure it out together and grow closer as we let each other get further apart. I don't want to be left to my own devices on my own, in the dark.

SAVE TO DRAFTS

[Lights up.]

Further reading (and borrowed lyrics) can be found in *Sex at Dawn* by Christopher Ryan and Cacilda Jethá; *How To Think More About Sex* by Alain de Botton; *Everybody Lies* by Seth Stephens-Davidowitz; *Man Disconnected* by Philip Zimbardo and Nikita D. Coulombe; *The Cyber Effect* by Mary Aiken; *Modern Romance* by Aziz Ansari and Eric Klinenberg; *Cat Sense* by John Bradshaw; *Future Sex* by Emily Witt; *Girls & Sex* by Peggy Orenstein; *Sexuality: All That Matters* by Louise Foxcroft and Dan Savage's *Savage Lovecast*.